What's for lunch?

Eggs

D0126855

© 1999 by Franklin Watts Ltd
96 Leonard Street
London
EC2A 4XD

First American edition 1999 by Franklin Watts/Children's Press
A Division of Grolier Publishing
90 Sherman Turnpike
Danbury, CT 06816

Editor: Samantha Armstrong
Series Designer: Kirstie Billingham
Designer: Jason Anscomb
Consultant: British Egg Information Service
Reading Consultant: Prue Goodwin, Reading and Language
Information Centre, Reading.

ISBN 0-516-21547-7

A catalog record for this book is available from the
Library of Congress

Visit Franklin Watts/Children's Press on the Internet at:
http://publishing.grolier.com

Printed in Hong Kong

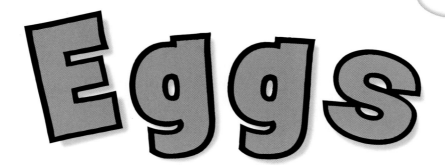

What's for lunch?

Eggs

Claire Llewellyn

CHILDREN'S PRESS®

A Division of Grolier Publishing

NEW YORK • LONDON • HONG KONG • SYDNEY
DANBURY, CONNECTICUT

4

Today we are having eggs for lunch.
Eggs contain **protein, vitamins,** and
minerals. They help us grow
and stay healthy.

We eat eggs laid by chickens, ducks, and turkeys.
All these birds are farmyard birds.
Another name for them is **poultry**.
They are usually kept on poultry farms.

Most often we eat the eggs of
female chickens, or hens.
Sometimes eggs have been **fertilized**
and **hatch** into baby chicks.
But the eggs we eat have not been fertilized,
so they could never hatch into chicks.

Hens' eggs can have white, brown, or speckled shells. It depends on the **breed** of hen.

On poultry farms, hens lay eggs
all through the year.
The farmer removes the eggs each day.

There are different kinds of poultry farms.
On **free-range** farms, hens wander outside.
They peck around looking for insects,
worms, roots, and leaves.
Free-range hens sleep in a henhouse.
The eggs are gathered together at the
henhouse and taken to the packing room.

Battery farms are another kind of
poultry farm.
The hens are kept inside cages,
with four or five hens in each cage.
The birds are given food and water
every few hours.
Their eggs are taken on a **conveyor belt**
to the packing room.

In the packing room,
the eggs are checked for cracks or faults.
The egg checkers use a special light to see
inside the eggs to make sure they are
safe to eat.
This is called **candling.**

The good eggs are sorted into different sizes
and packed into boxes.
The boxes are labeled to show where
and when the eggs were laid and the date
by which they should be eaten.
Some stores like their eggs to be stamped
so that customers can see
if they are fresh enough to use.

The eggs are then delivered to farm markets, stores and supermarkets.

Eggs are usually sold in cartons of twelve, or a **dozen**.

Sometimes boxes of six eggs, or half a dozen, are available.

Any eggs that are cracked or oddly shaped are sold to food manufacturers.
At the factory, the eggs are broken open and specially treated to keep them fresh.
This is called **pasteurization.**

Pasteurized eggs are added to noodles, cake mixes, and ice cream.

They are also used in some paints, soaps, and shampoos.

Eggs are eaten in many different ways.
They can be used to make a cake. They can be fried in a frying pan.

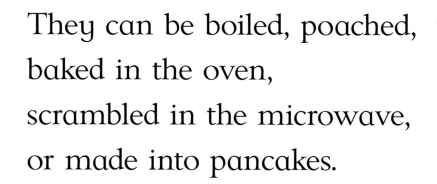

They can be boiled, poached,
baked in the oven,
scrambled in the microwave,
or made into pancakes.

Sometimes we use only part of the egg –
the **yolk** or the **white**.
Meringues are made by whisking
egg whites with sugar.
Eggs are one of the most useful foods.
They are delicious and good for you, too.

Glossary

battery a type of poultry farm where hens are kept in cages

breed a particular type of animal

candling the way that eggs are checked to see if they are safe to eat. Each egg is held up to a special light

conveyor belt a moving belt that carries items such as eggs from one place to another

dozen twelve of any object, especially eggs

fertilized when an egg contains a baby chick

free-range a type of poultry farm where hens wander around and peck freely

hatch when baby birds break out of their shells

minerals   materials found in rocks and also in food. Minerals help us stay healthy

pasteurization   a way of treating eggs and other foods to kill any harmful bacteria and make them last longer

poultry   the name for all types of birds that are raised on farms

protein   something found in foods, such as eggs, that makes our bodies strong

vitamins   something found in foods such as fruit, vegetables, and eggs that keeps us healthy

white   the see-through part of an egg that turns white when it is cooked

yolk   the yellow part of an egg

Index

Picture credits: FLPA: 7 (W Adams/Sunset); Holt Studios International: 8 (Micheal Mayer), 10 (Sarah Rowland), 13 (Nigel Cattlin), 15 (Julia Chalmers), 16 (Inga Spence), 19 (David Burton), 20 (Nigel Cattlin); Panos Pictures: 23 (David Sprague). Franklin Watts Photo Library P9, 24. 25 top, 26-27; Steve Shott cover, backcover; All other photographs Tim Ridley, Wells Street Studios, London. **With thanks to Nyran Sri-Pathmanathan and Charlotte Trundley.**